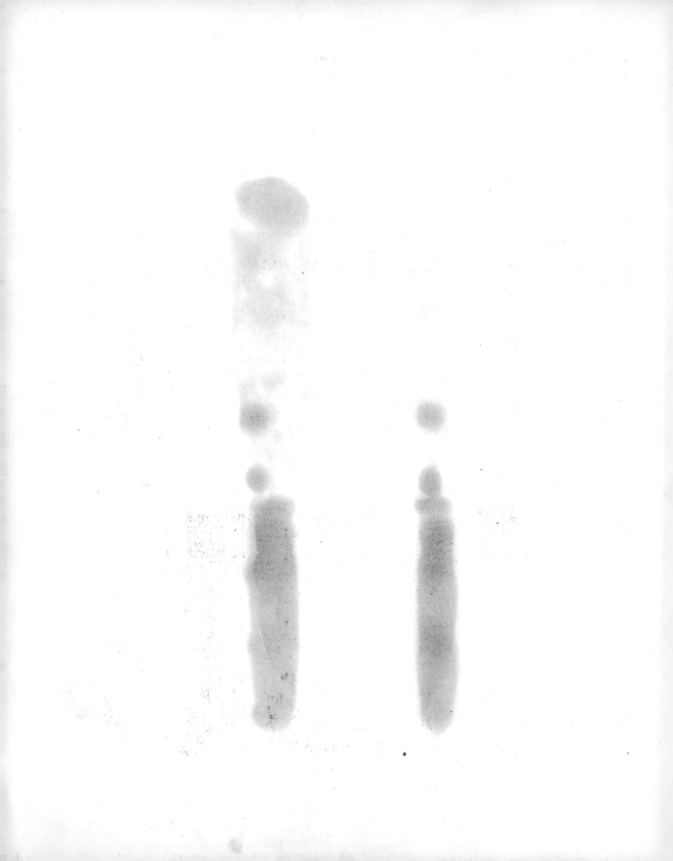

SECRETS OF THE *VENUS'S FLY TRAP*

JEROME WEXLER

DODD, MEAD & COMPANY * NEW YORK

Library of Congress Cataloging in Publication Data

Wexler, Jerome.
    Secrets of the Venus's fly trap.

    SUMMARY: Details the growth of the Venus's Fly Trap,
its reaction to various "foods," and how to care for it
at home.

    1. Venus's-flytrap—Juvenile literature. [1. Venus's-
flytrap. 2. Insectivorous plants] I. Title.
QK495.D76W49   635.9′33121   80-2775
ISBN 0-396-07941-5   AACR1

SECRETS OF THE VENUS'S FLY TRAP

THE TRAP

This is a maple leaf. It has two main parts, the large flat area and the stem. The large flat area is called the blade. The stem is called the petiole.

This is the leaf of a Venus's Fly Trap. It also has two parts: the blade and the petiole.

With the help of sunlight, maple leaves change gases from the air, nutrients from the earth, and water into food for the maple tree. In order for this to happen, the roots of the maple tree must first suck the water and nutrients from the soil and send them to the leaves.

With the help of sunlight, the leaves on the Venus's Fly Trap also change gases, nutrients, and water into food for the plant. But the Venus's Fly Trap gets very little of its nutrients from the soil.

Venus's Fly Traps grow naturally only in a small area of North and South Carolina. There the land is low and boggy. The acid soil is composed mostly of sand and peat. It does not contain the nutrients the plant needs. How does the plant survive?

The Venus's Fly Trap catches insects and eats them. It takes the nutrients it needs from the insects it eats.

The blade opens wide, like a landing field, inviting insects to visit. And what a visit!

On the inner surface of the blade are some short, stiff hairs. These are called sensitive hairs, or trigger hairs. There may be as many as a dozen, but usually there are six, three on each lobe (side). They are arranged so that a good-sized insect cannot walk across the surface of the blade without touching them.

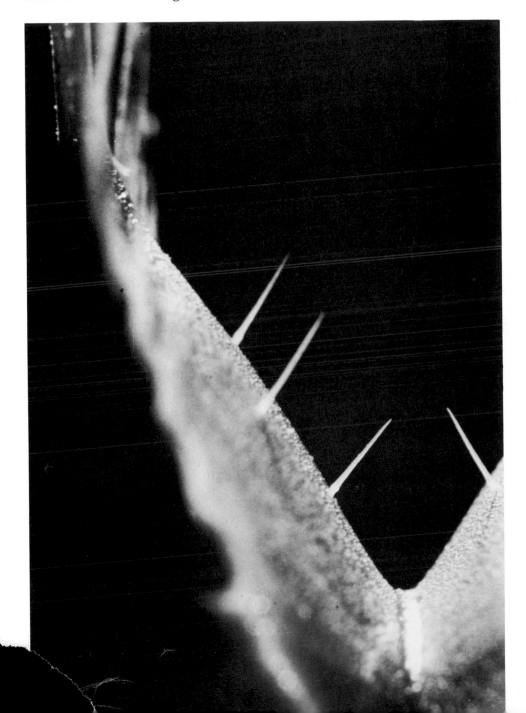

Whenever anything—a finger, an insect, a blade of grass, even (sometimes) a raindrop—touches the trigger hairs enough to bend them, the blade folds up. The two lobes snap together, trapping whatever is inside.

On a very warm day, the trap will close if only one trigger hair is touched. But most of the time, at least two hairs must be bent, one after the other, or one hair can be touched twice. On very cold days, many trigger hairs must be bent before the trap will close.

Venus's Fly Traps were discovered over two hundred years ago, and they have fascinated people ever since. For decades, so many thousands of plants were dug up that eventually they became scarce and were placed on the endangered list. Today, very few "wild" plants are harvested. Almost all the Venus's Fly Traps that are sold around the world are grown commercially in greenhouses.

Venus's Fly Traps can be raised indoors and outdoors. They often come with instructions that say that plants raised outdoors will capture enough insects to stay healthy, but plants raised indoors must be fed small amounts of raw hamburger. Let's keep some plants outdoors and some indoors and try to feed an indoor plant a little hamburger.

As soon as the meat touches the trigger hairs, the trap closes around it.
It happens in less than a second.

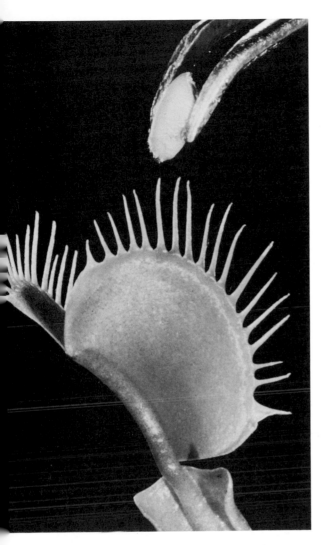

What else will this amazing plant accept? A seed of wheat?

A small piece of gravel from the aquarium?

The traps snap shut over the seed and the gravel as soon as their trigger hairs are touched.

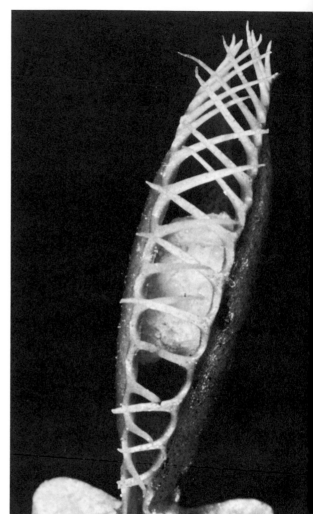

But twelve hours later they have opened enough to "spit" out their food.

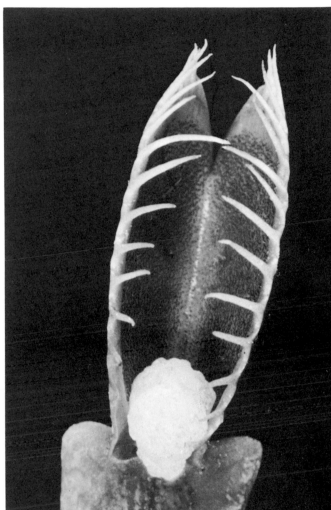

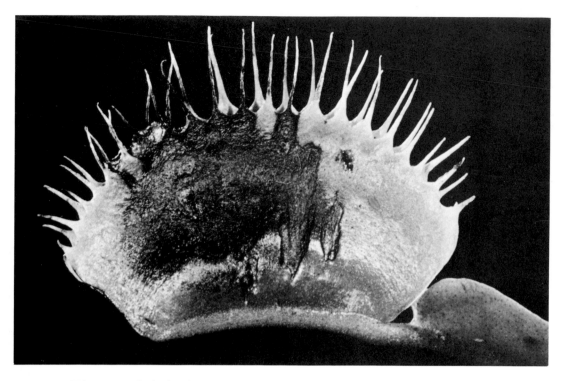

The trap fed the hamburger did not spit it out. The piece was too big for the trap to close completely, and the warmth of the room melted the fatty part of the meat. It oozed all over the blade and the petiole. After six days the trap started to rot. There was an awful smell inside.

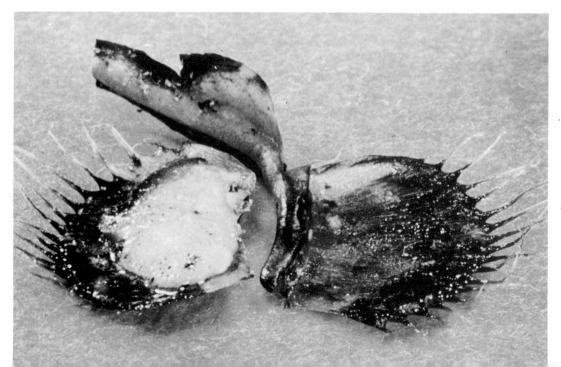

One day, a trap on one of the outdoor plants caught a kind of spider
known as a daddy longlegs. Six days later, the trap started to rot.

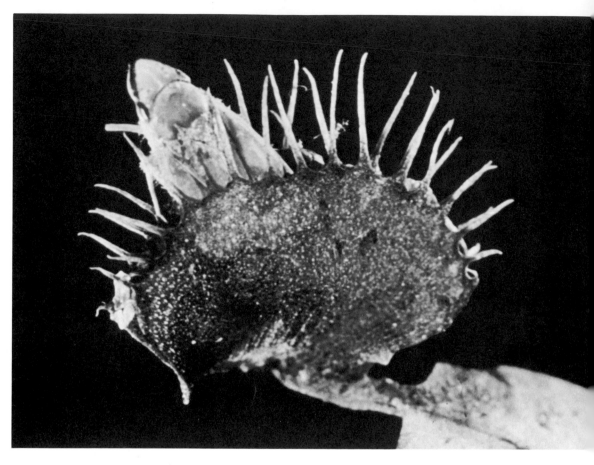

Another trap caught a leafhopper. A week later it, too, started to rot. Maybe the Venus's Fly Trap doesn't eat insects after all?

Then one day a trap on an outdoor plant was closed. Twelve days later it opened. Inside was what looked like a fly.

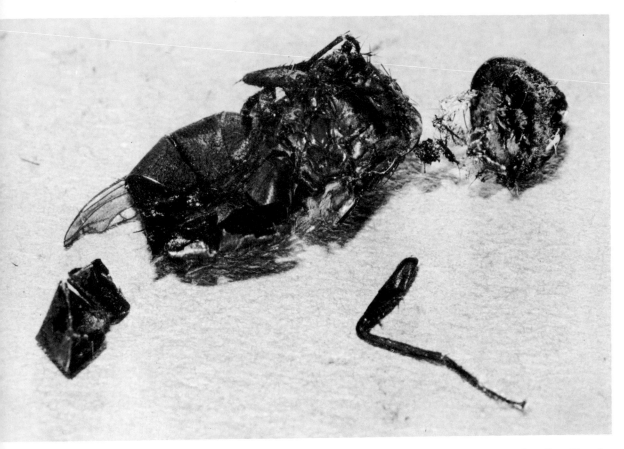

It was really only the hard outer shell (exoskeleton) of the fly. Crushing it showed that all the soft parts of the insect were gone. The Venus's Fly Trap had eaten the soft inner tissues. No harm had come to the trap.

What went wrong those other times?

Let's feed a few live insects to other traps and watch what happens. We'll use the kind of wasps called yellow jackets.

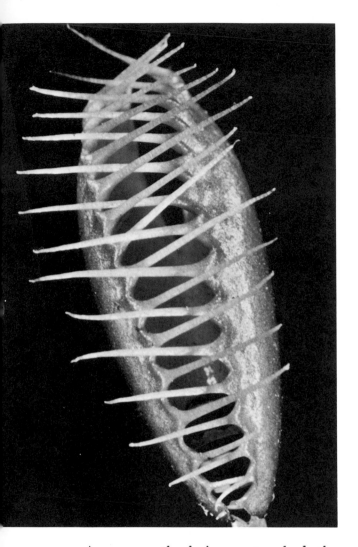 

As soon as the hairs are touched, the trap closes—but not all the way. It is thought that the trap stays partly open for a while to allow very small insects to leave. These insects are too small for the plant to get much nourishment from eating them. But the long "fingers" (called cilia) interlace to keep large insects from escaping.

Within minutes, the trap resumes its closing action, forming a hollow tomb for the doomed insect.

The rims of the two halves eventually come together with great force. They make an airtight seal that will keep the digestive fluids in the trap.

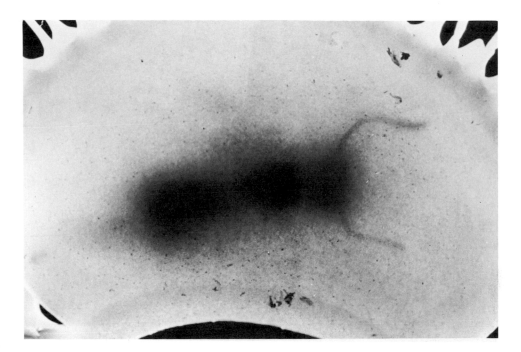

The man who first named the plant many years ago thought that the stiff trigger hairs acted as spears and killed the insect as the trap closed. But hold a trap that has just caught an insect up to a bright light. The live insect can be seen moving about inside the trap. It may move for just a few minutes or for as long as an hour.

Can you see the way the yellow jacket has changed position inside the trap?

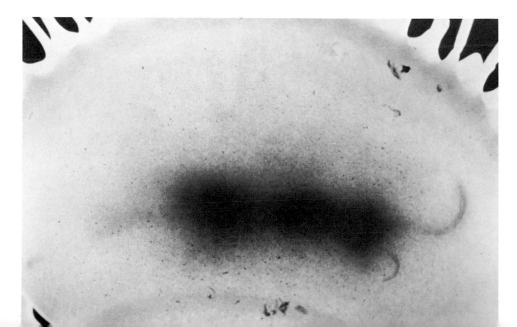

About twelve hours later the trap begins to constrict. The cilia stretch upright.

Sometimes the cilia unlace. Now it is possible to see how tightly the rims are sealed. If an insect gets caught only partway in the trap, as the daddy longlegs and the leafhopper did, the pressure between the rims can be enough to kill it. But the insect's body will prevent the trap from making an airtight seal.

Bacteria and molds on the insect's body start to make it decay. The decay will spread to the trap, too.

Now one side of the trap collapses inward. Except where the insect lies, the inner surfaces of the trap touch each other.

This collapsing action is called the narrowing phase. During the narrowing phase, the space within the trap becomes smaller and smaller, and the trap begins to make digestive fluid.

This trap has been cut away to show what is happening.

Forty-eight hours have passed. Another trap has been cut away to show what is happening. Now the yellow jacket seems to float in a sea of fluid that is the color and consistency of honey. This is the digestive fluid, and it dissolves the soft parts of the insect. It is not strong enough to dissolve the tough exoskeleton.

Once the insect's soft inner tissues are digested, the plant reabsorbs the digestive fluid, and the trap opens. The exoskeleton can be carried off by a gust of wind or washed away by rain.

A Venus's Fly Trap needs somewhere between five and twenty days to digest its catch. The time depends on the size of the catch, the age of the trap, the number of times the trap has gone through this cycle before, and also the temperature of the air.

We have just seen a Venus's Fly Trap digest a live insect. Why wouldn't it digest a seed or a bit of hamburger? Can the plant somehow tell the difference between food that is alive and food that is not?

Let's feed part of a dead insect to another trap and see what happens. The abdomen of a yellow jacket will do nicely, for it contains a large amount of soft tissue.

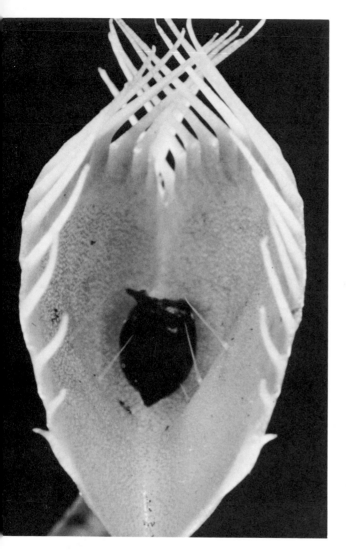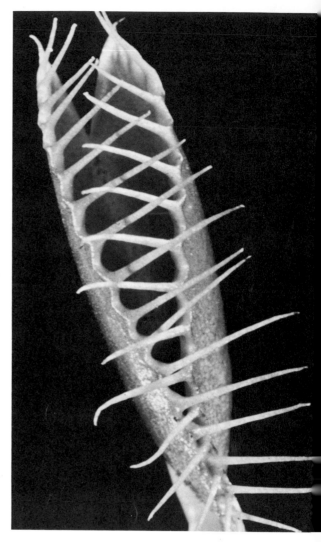

Once again, as soon as the abdomen touches the trigger hairs, the trap starts to close.

Twelve hours later it has opened slightly. But it does not open wide to discard its catch, as it did with the seed and the gravel. Perhaps the trap can tell that there is food inside. Yet it cannot go ahead and begin the various stages of digestion.

The problem is probably not the food, since we just saw the plant consume a live yellow jacket. What did the live insect do that the abdomen by itself did not? Of course! The live insect struggled inside the closed trap.

Let's run a new test using another yellow jacket abdomen and another trap. This time, after the trap has closed, let's squeeze the trap gently for two or three minutes to imitate the struggles of a live insect.

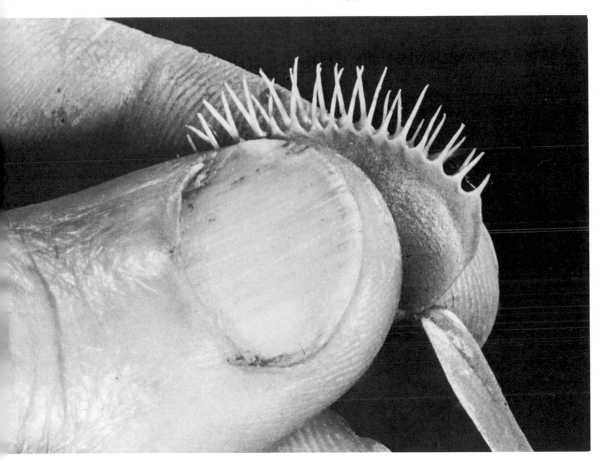

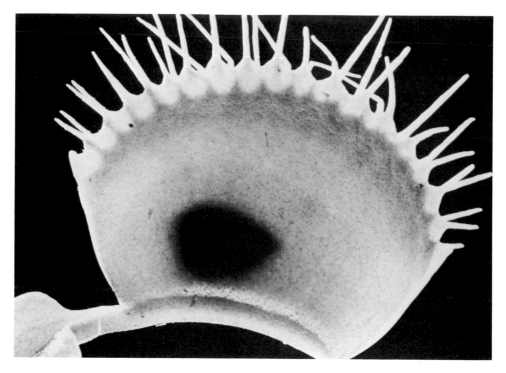

It worked. This time the trap sealed itself and remained closed for eleven days.

When the trap reopened, the abdomen looked the way it had when it was dropped in. But crushing it showed that the plant had digested the soft tissue inside.

A trap will snap shut any time its trigger hairs are touched. Once a trap is shut, movement within the trap tells the plant that whatever is caught is alive. This movement within the closed trap is the signal that causes the trap to begin to constrict and narrow, in preparation for digestion. Without this movement signal, the trap simply opens and releases what is inside.

If we use this signal, will the Venus's Fly Trap digest a small piece of meat? Let's try a piece of lean beef, since the hamburger made a mess of the plant before.

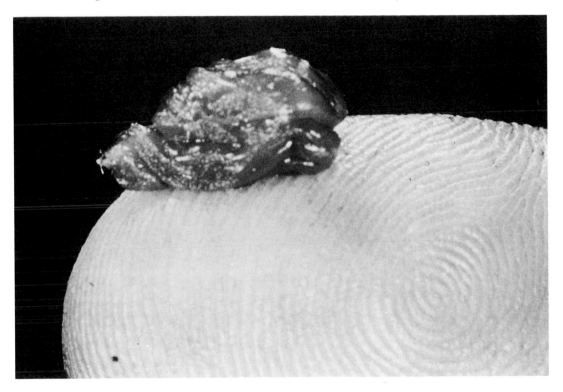

Sure enough. The trap neither spit the meat out nor rotted. When it opened nine days later, all the meat had been digested. Nothing was left. Now we know how to feed plants any time of the year.

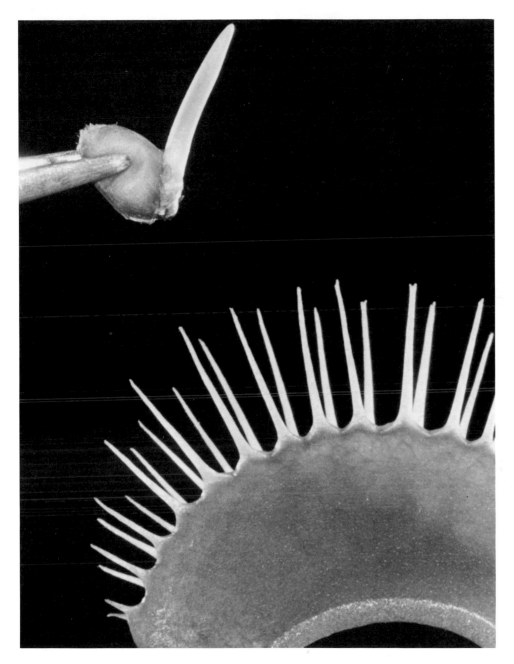

What about using the movement signal with a seed of wheat? After the trap was massaged, it remained closed for six days. When it opened, the seed had sprouted! Somehow the moisture of the digestive fluid allowed the seed to begin to grow, just as though it were in the dark, rich earth.

THE PLANT

We've seen how the Venus's Fly Trap eats insects, but how does the plant grow? The stem of a Venus's Fly Trap is called a rhizome. Rhizome is a fancy name given to a plant stem that grows just beneath the surface of the soil instead of straight up into the air. The rhizome of the Venus's Fly Trap grows for as long as the plant is alive. This growth causes the plant to slowly "walk" away from the spot in which it was planted.

In this photo, the growing tip of the rhizome is on the far right. Only here can new leaves form. As they form, the rhizome grows a little longer to support them. The oldest leaf begins to die off, and the part of the rhizome that supported it dies off, too. With each new leaf, the center of the plant shifts toward the growing end. A Venus's Fly Trap can be planted in the exact center of a flower pot, but two or three years later it will be found growing at the edge of the pot.

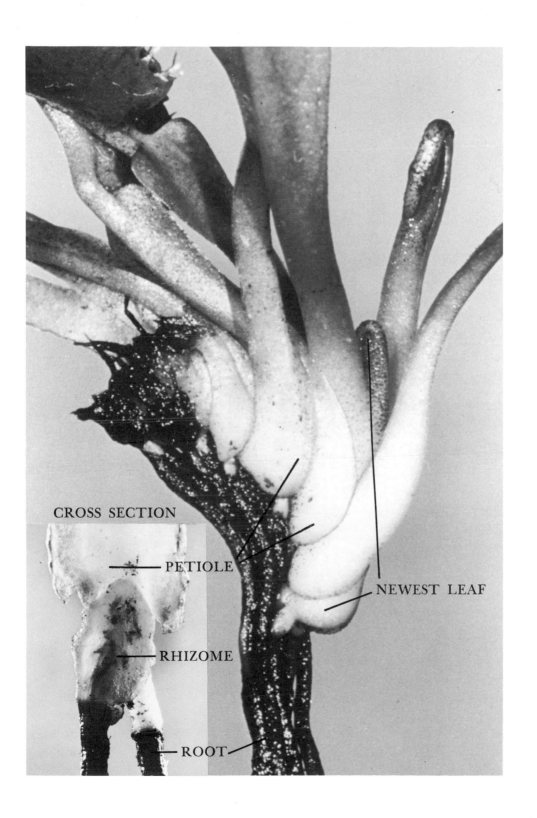

CROSS SECTION

PETIOLE

RHIZOME

ROOT

NEWEST LEAF

Above ground, the plant takes the form of a rosette. Each new leaf tucks itself in between some of the older leaves and breaks through the soil near the center of the plant.

The two parts of the leaf, the petiole and the blade, do not develop at the same rate. The petiole develops first.

 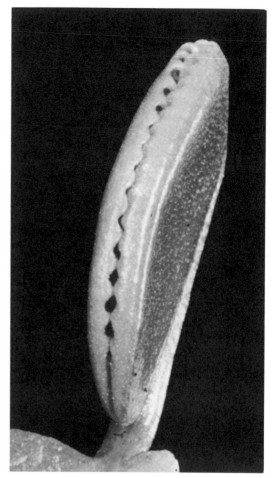

Then the blade grows rapidly.

The sides of the trap fill out, and the two halves begin to separate.

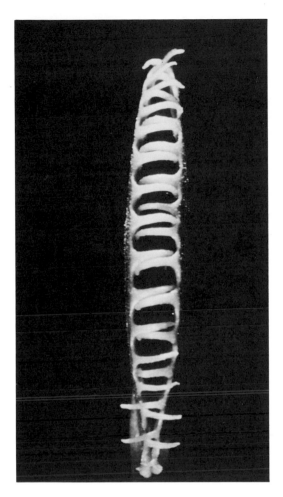

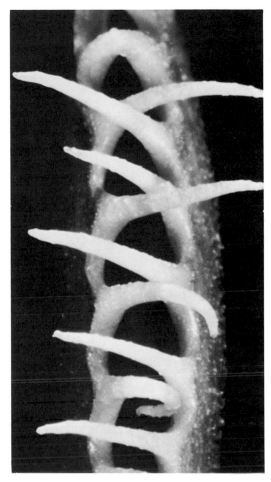

The cilia untuck themselves.

They pop out interlaced, just as they will be when the trap captures an insect.

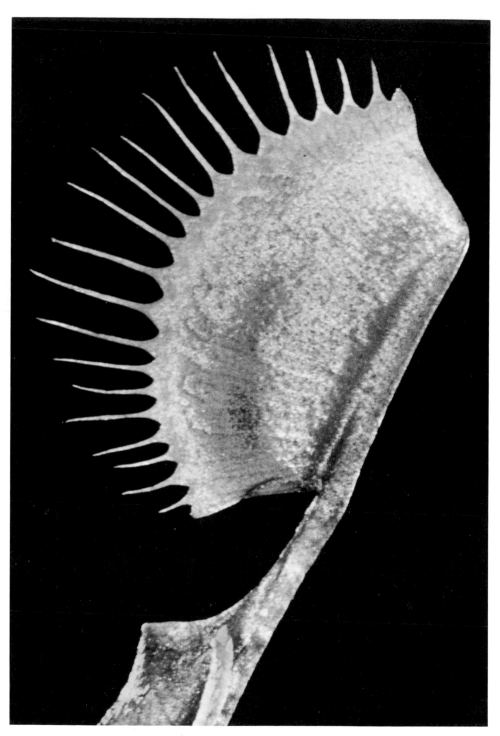

Each lobe has between eighteen and twenty-one cilia.

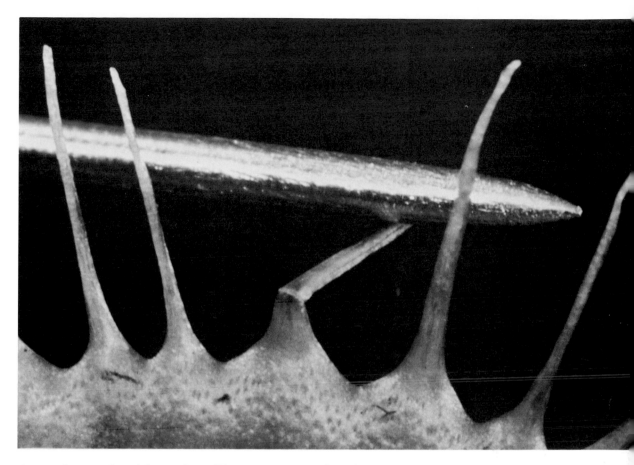

A gentle touch with a pin will cause one to break . . .

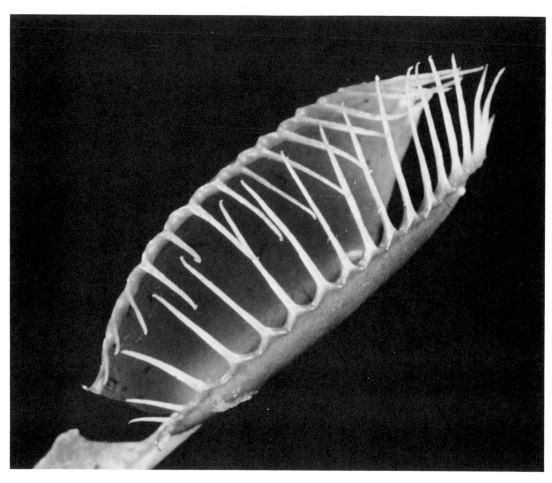

... but together they are strong enough to keep an insect from escaping
the trap.

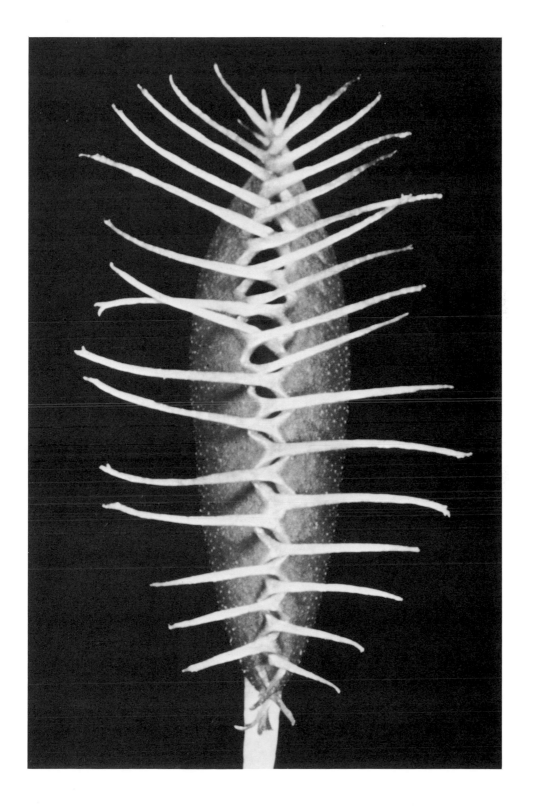

A narrow band runs along the rim just below the cilia. This band is called the "perfume band." Occasionally droplets appear on the perfume "glands." There is no noticeable odor, however, nor do these traps seem to attract many nectar-feeding insects. The inner surface of the trap can vary in color from a dark green to a bright red. Some growers believe that the bright red traps, which look very much like pieces of raw beef, draw flesh-eating insects to the plant.

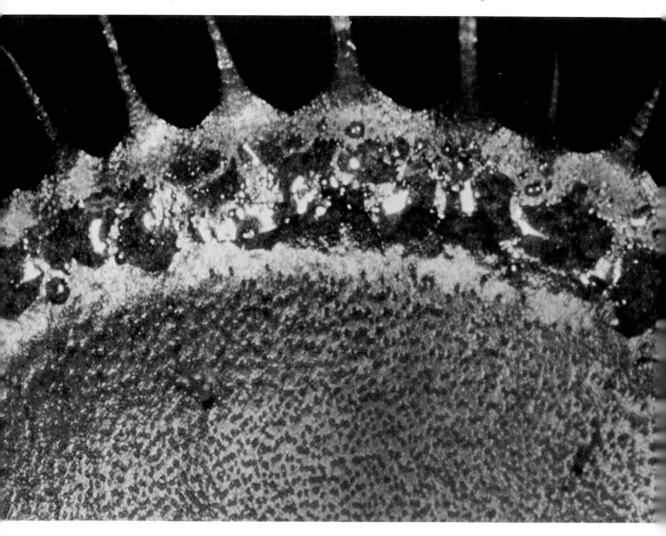

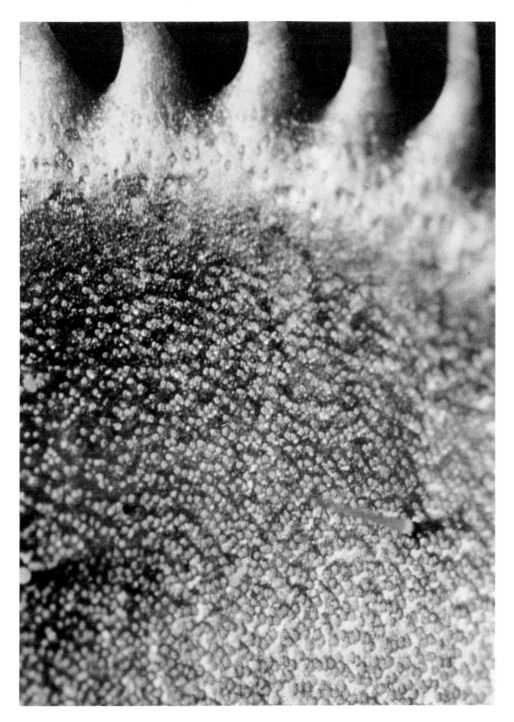

Most of the surface of the trap is covered with digestive glands. These glands produce the digestive fluid and then reabsorb it.

REPRODUCTION

Like many other plants, a Venus's Fly Trap can make seeds from which new plants will grow. But to make seeds, the plant must first make flowers. The flowers attract insects, and the insects, almost by accident, help the plant make seeds.

The plant has a clever way to keep these insects safe from its deadly leaves. Can you see what it is? The flowers sit high above the traps at the top of a very long stem.

Early in the spring the flower stem, called a scape, breaks through the soil in the center of the rosette.

When the scape is as tall as it will get (sometimes a foot high), the top bursts open. It is filled with buds.

Each bud opens into a flower with five pale green petals. Each flower also has many stamens full of pollen grains. In the center of all the stamens is something called a pistil.

For a seed to form, pollen from a stamen must somehow reach the pistil. The pollen can come from stamens on the same flower or on another flower of the same plant, or even from a flower on a different Venus's Fly Trap plant.

How does the pollen reach the pistil? Insects help. Deep inside the flowers are drops of a very sweet liquid called nectar. Many insects like this nectar and stop by the flowers to get it. As they walk down into the flowers trying to reach the nectar, the hairs on their bodies become coated with pollen. If they happen to bump into the pistil, some of the pollen grains brush off onto it.

If the plants are indoors, and no insects can reach the flowers, someone else must help the plant.

It really is quite simple. A stamen full of pollen grains is removed with a pair of tweezers . . .

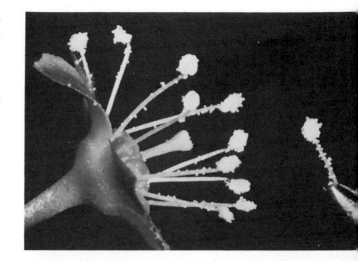

. . . and dabbed against the tip of the pistil.

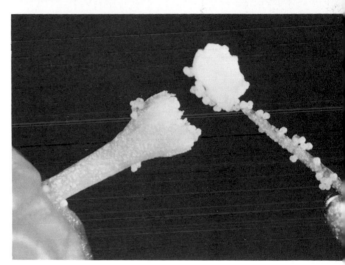

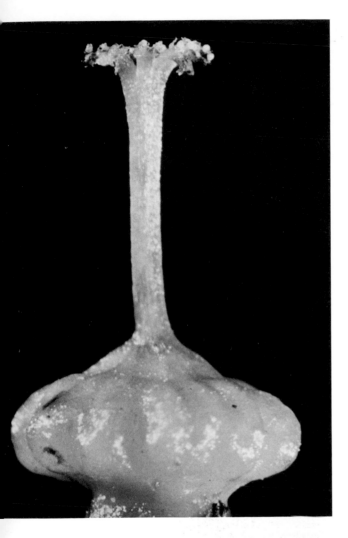

The pistil is made up of three parts. At the base is the ovary, a large swollen structure that contains unfertilized seeds (called ovules). At the top is a stigma, which receives the pollen. In between is a long, slender style.

Once a pollen grain reaches the stigma, it sends a pollen tube down into the style to unite with an ovule in the ovary. This uniting is called fertilization. When an ovule is fertilized, it starts to become a seed.

The flowers on the Venus's Fly Trap are quite small. The ovary at the base of the pistil sits so deep inside the flower that most of the petals must be removed to see it.

After fertilization, the ovary enlarges. Nothing else seems to happen for about six to eight weeks. Then, almost overnight, the ovary turns black. The seeds are ripe.

Each flower produces eight to twelve seeds. Since there may be a dozen flowers on a scape, and often two scapes on a plant, one Venus's Fly Trap can produce quite a large number of seeds.

The seeds are tiny—even smaller than the head of a pin. They must be planted right away or stored in the refrigerator. The period at the end of this sentence was made with a Venus's Fly Trap seed.

The seeds sprout two weeks to a month after they are planted.

The first pair of leaves look nothing like the regular leaves. They are called seed leaves.

But the leaves that develop next are adult in every respect, right down to their tiny new traps!

The Venus's Fly Trap, like many other plants, can produce new plants another way, without making seeds. New Venus's Fly Traps can be sprouted from the rhizome and the leaves of a plant that is already growing. Sometimes, especially in spring, a rhizome will produce one or more branches. A Venus's Fly Trap seldom has more than seven mature leaves at one time. If a plant has more than seven, it is likely that the rhizome has produced a new branch.

Each branch will have its own growing point, producing its own group
of leaves.

The branches can be separated from
the "mother" plant and then planted
in their own pots.

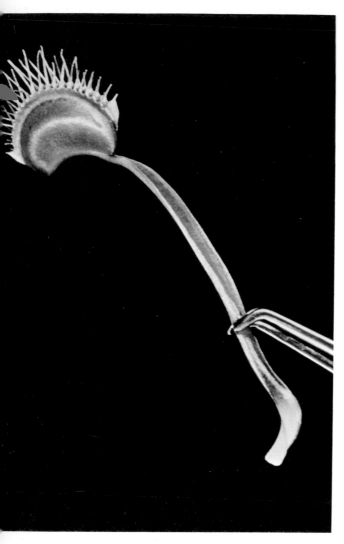

A Venus's Fly Trap can be "forced" to produce new plants by removing the three outermost leaves, taking a little of the rhizome with each leaf. Each leaf is then laid flat on some sphagnum moss with the last half-inch of the petiole tucked into the moss.

As the days go by, the part of the leaf above the moss dies off . . .

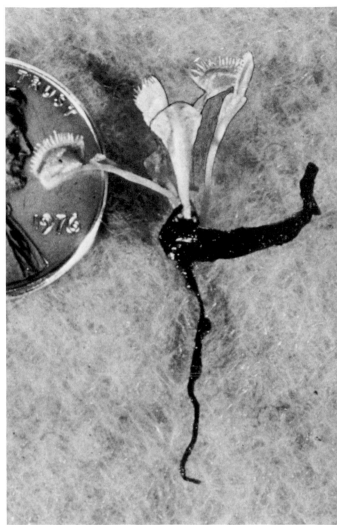

. . . but the portion under the moss will produce roots, and then . . .

. . . a whole new plant.

GROWING YOUR OWN

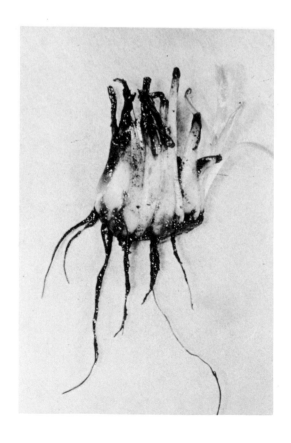

Raising your own Venus's Fly Trap plants is both fun and easy—easy because the plants require just a few simple things: wet roots; high humidity; poor soil, on the acid side; full sunlight.

Plants can often be obtained from local plant nurseries or plant stores. They can also be gotten from mail-order plant nurseries that specialize in carnivorous plants. (*Carnivorous* means "flesh eating." Carnivorous plants are also called *insectivorous*, which means "insect eating.") You can find the names and addresses of these firms by checking the classified section of a gardening magazine. They are listed under the heading "Carnivorous Plants."

Plants come in the active growing state or as "bulbs" (the rhizomes plus the roots). To grow a bulb, just plant it—root end down and deep enough that the top of the bulb is even with the soil surface. Place it in a warm, sunny area.

An ideal soil mix for carnivorous plants consists of one part good soil (such as African Violet soil mix), four parts sphagnum moss, and five parts washed sand. *Never* add lime or fertilizer to the soil! If you do not want to mix your own soil, prepared soil can be purchased from a mail-order nursery.

For indoor growing, where the air is dry, containers with a large volume and a small opening are ideal. The glass walls and the small opening help keep moisture around the plant.

Another way to increase the humidity is to place the potted plant in a larger container and then partly cover it with a piece of glass or Plexiglas. Be sure you don't cover more than two-thirds of the top, because the air must be able to circulate. Keep at least a half-inch of water in the large container at all times.

This arrangement is good for both indoor or outdoor use, although when it rains, the water level may rise above the pot and flood the leaves. This won't harm the plant, but the leaves do get messy. A small hole drilled into the large container, about an inch below the rim of the flowerpot, will prevent this.

Small aquariums also work well. Indoors, place the aquarium in the sunniest window of the house or under a grow lamp that's on for about sixteen hours a day. Outdoors, place the aquarium so that the plants get full sun for most of the day. Never let the soil dry out. Tap water is usually all right, but rainwater is better. If it rains and the container fills, don't worry. The plants can grow for months under water with no harm.

There are approximately five hundred species of carnivorous plants throughout the world. There are also a great many people who are interested in these plants, and they have formed a society to gather and share information. Their address is:

International Carnivorous Plant Society
c/o The Fullerton Arboretum
California State University
Fullerton, California 92634

They do not sell plants, but each year in the March issue of their quarterly publication, they list the names and addresses of plant nurseries throughout the world from which carnivorous plants can be purchased.